hawakal creative

Scrawls and Scribbles

Sharmila Ray

HAWAKAL PUBLISHERS

Published by: Bitan Chakraborty, on behalf of **Hawakal Publishers**, 185, Kali Temple Road, Nimta, Calcutta 700049, India.

First edition: November, 2016

Printed at: S. P. Communications , Raja Dinendra Chandra Street, Calcutta 700009.

Contact: Bitan Chakraborty (Founder, Hawakal)
Email: info@hawakal.com

Copyright © 2016 Sharmila Ray

All rights reserved. No part of this publication may be reproduced or transmitted (other than for purposes of review/critique) in any form or by any means, electronic or mechanical, including photocopy, recording, or any information storage and retrieval system without prior permission in writing from the publisher or the copyright holder where applicable. The author asserts her moral right to be identified as the author of his work.

Cover concept and design: Sudhangsu

ISBN-13: 97893-85782-90-9

Price: INR One Hundred and Eighty (Rs. 180/- only)

To my mother, **_Snigdha Roy_**, who introduced me to a world of words.

Acknowledgements

Some of these poems have been published in the *Journal* (Poetry Society India), *World Poetry Yearbook 2013,* eds, Choi Lai Shung and Zhang Zhi, *The Seventh Quarry,* Autumn 2014, Swansea Poetry Magazine, Wales, UK, *Indo Australian Anthology Of Contemporary Poets,* eds, Sunil Sharma and Bob Harle, *Indian Literature* (Sahitya Akademi's Bi-Monthly Journal) .

I wish to thank my family for always giving me the space I need for writing.

My friends for being there.

Bitan Chakraborty of Hawakal Publishers for having faith in me and without whom this book would not have been possible.

Thank You

Sometimes, I ask myself do I need to write a foreword or an introduction or whatever you might call, to a collection of my poems? Honestly, I think it is redundant. For, this page is not a classroom where I would try to convey my inner workings in prose. As far as I am concerned poetry is a universe composed of infinite number of sentences, hallucinating sentences, meditative sentences, adoring sentences, impenetrable sentences, sentences which threaten our composure and, therefore, our very existence . Words squabbling in the confined corridors of sentences greedy for combination. Seen from this perspective, the universe becomes a labyrinth of shadow and light where reality and fantasy form a lattice pattern. It rests on an individual as to how she or he will decode this labyrinth.

Sharmila Ray
Kolkata
October 2016

Contents

- Words 11
- Small 12
- Alphabets 13
- Alternatives 14
- My morning 15
- Childhood totems 16
- Came up with 17
- Journey 18
- Fragments from a diary 19
- An inaudible cry 20
- Because 21
- Burnt continent 22
- Day break 23
- Distances 24
- Finding oneself 25
- Delhi 2010 26
- Forgetting is easy 27
- If only 28
- Sarnath 29
- For freido calho 30
- I wonder 31
- Oh alexandria 32
- Coffee bar 34
- Mundane little things 35
- Ruins 36
- 37 Song of mohenjo daro
- 38 My valentine
- 39 Sleep smell
- 40 Sea shell
- 41 The written word
- 42 Sea
- 43 Stop
- 44 Tropes for the intelligent man
- 48 Train leaves
- 49 Sunday night bliss
- 50 Song
- 51 T3
- 52 Once again
- 53 Trying times
- 54 Turnip
- 55 Veiled
- 56 Water drops
- 58 Politician
- 59 She II
- 60 Sentences
- 61 Loosing colour
- 62 Pilgrims
- 63 Night
- 64 Voyage
- 66 Writing a poem is not easy

WORDS

Alphabets jumble words mingle
as I start writing a poem.
Long lines of words.

As I go on talking to you
 they are words compressed.
As you listen to me
they are words reticent.

My thoughts are silent words.

Your smile
a wide beautiful word.

And words have colours too-
 coral, topaz, cerulean.

Words breathe, words speak.
Sometimes, dust settles on words
and they become heavy engraving on hearts.

But when words lose sound
and become deep seas within us,
then the secrets of the universe
are told in whispers.

SMALL

My world is small
you may call it colourless,
you can add all your comments,
commas and full stops.
But I have no desire to think.
You can feed all the clouds in my
world with crumpled blotting paper,
still it wouldn't make a difference.
You can dress the streets with swathes of
supermarkets and high rises, throttle silence
with metal sounds and try to do whatever
satisfies you.
In fact, make the universe a prison house.

But remember
green and summer squirrels leapfrogged here and
everything is an islet in the lucid sea of change.

ALPHABETS

Alphabets march to enter my heart
but an ancient wind stops them.
They get lost
they die
without forming a word.
However, in the evening they return
with kites
with birds.
Coloured alphabets
sitting arrogantly on my desk
deriding me.
Alphabets mist of my armpits.
Alphabets the cotton stretched
over my breasts.
Alphabets the invisible horizon.

I'm swept.

In the sense-space of my thought
alphabets grow again on their own
as do the fern
much like the nail on your finger.
Alphabets mother of words.
Alphabets word-forest.
And if we do loose ourselves
in the forest, it is exactly then
that we find our voice.

ALTERNATIVES

I think it would be interesting to tell you about the problems I have not yet resolved. The moment I try to solve them, like sudden hell my world disintegrates and all the possible variants become more distant like foam on the edge of an unknown planet. My devouring obsession paralyses me and my alternatives like white ghosts blend in with moist rain. But I don't give up and from fleeting shadows forms emerge-

Can poetry turn into a trail inviting to the other side where huge Van Gogh sun burns copper-lemon and some god of antiquity wantonly eyes me, flirts with me between the narrow lanes of housing complex?

Can all the sparkles of the day make me write poetry if my fingers are dipped in inane canon?

Can all the goodbyes be given a bath of holy oil so that they shine and seem sacrosanct?

Believe me, I have pondered long, but always ended up in an oppressive bake-house, the flour spreading taking root in my throat choking me as I anticipate winter.

MY MORNING

Every morning I sit here
the pinewood casting a mellow glow-
My room with orderly and disorderly books
slanting, pilled up or straight lined in bookshelves.
Before I've a chance to do anything, the books in unison
call out 'let's refresh your mind'. Before I've a chance to
protest they start conversing-

Sometimes, Borges leaps out of
Aleph and weaves a fantastic story of a
 universe that lies hidden inside a stone pillar.
And at other times Gilgamesh takes me to the edge of a
 nation extinct long ago. Caught up in the wreck of languages
I try to understand the unsung subtexts-

Calvino among reeds, his wet feet draped with
green algae, creating patterns on the floor. Blue Dragon flies
appear only to vanish. I get up pick up a book, the words emerge
sticky with nectar, crawl all over my body and sting.

CHILDHOOD TOTEMS

What happened to us, to our friends?
I have imagined it all…
The megapixels freezing and then
suddenly exploding in rage-
black purple black.

Fractures thread the playground and
strange creatures-totems of childhood
lie wounded. They look at us curiously
to the fading innocence.
Meanwhile, with our mouths vitriolic,
our eyes screwed we stretch grey fingers
to daub poison on their palms, then go home
to begin another day in a narrow format.

CAME UP WITH

I dreamt of sea
and came up with waves
I dreamt of sky
and came up with stars
I dreamt of earth
and got myself greened
I dreamt of words
and found a voice.

JOURNEY

I'm trying to find a piece of land
far off from the smell of
Temple
Church
Mosque
with a single green leaf and a
half-open flower, with eyes
 mirroring celestial shadow and
teeth brushed clean of stained frenzy,
smelling of nutmeg and ripe guava.
But where do I start?
The centre is ever receding as one
twilight trail joins another,
leaving no trace, only the feel of
soft moss and crushed grain.
A sandpapered moon weakly casts
its shadow over quiet things.

Indeed!

But still I search,
take another step.
For I firmly believe the land
is just about the corner-
virgin, housing unending light
in bright torrents.

FRAGMENTS FROM A DIARY

She opens the day like a page from her diary. The morning sun pale, with diffused gold-spread stretch and moments grow on her window sill. Hours lean unobtrusively on hours. She observes the little jacket embroidered with peacocks neatly folded lying on a chair. She dusts off the furniture, puts chairs back in their place and sits nonplussed. The day crumbles into afternoon.

She pulls the curtains back. The sun beams fragmented into oblongs and ovals stream through window panes. The room behind her is a slit of amber and still harbours traces of last night. Thirsty sparrows sit on her just watered flower pots. Muffled sounds of coughing taxis float by. She takes a shower. Entangled with lavender and aloe she towel dries herself.

She rises to turn on the light. The evening pushes through a multi-layered alchemy of dos and don'ts. She doesn't feel like turning on the television. Violence deliberated in the boxy lighted space of security. Her teeth closing on an apple, take pleasure in the slow oozing of the tawny liquid. Her eyes scan the horizon's fluid contour making her a wanderer of clouds.

She pulls the curtains together. Over her landscape a translucent haze appear setting the rhythm of the night. The sky turns metallic indigo with spotlight- stars for company. Somewhere an owl screeches. The sound reverberates softly against the solid wall of her flat. Cut by the shadows of trees the whys and wherefores disintegrate. All that remains is life free flowing in spite of hiatus.

AN INAUDIBLE CRY

Are we messengers of god or ghost invisible,
charging each other in the dark night
like a raving mad man?
As if to convince ourselves we clothe the black venom
in a seductive dark voice.
We play games with the sound of a rattle snake for
company.
And strangely, when a north wind blows, pushing aside the
moth eaten curtain, we see clammy fat, binding our
hearts,
 squeezing all the depths, till there is nothing
to flush down the veins.

Possessed, we have nothing, not even our shadows,
but, an inaudible cry only.

BECAUSE

Because we care
the uncurtained unfurnished room
of ours in the lazy afternoon
is matt gold and
we're two black dots
washed in salt and saliva
on the same pillow together.

Because we care
the shadows under muted lamp
become frescoes
and you give me your memories
and I promise you my tomorrows.

Because we care
our nakedness under coverlet
is reassuring, while we touch
each others fear.

Because we care
the stars, the everydayness and
those friends of ours are there,
but in another hemisphere and
we cross the need to be exceptional.

BURNT CONTINENT

Sometimes, by a quirk of fate in certain landscapes the
                               sun clings to the sky,
its lemon tentacles hot and acid. Down below her
                               tattooed skin blisters and
summer refuses to leave her, dehydrating the ancient
                               rhythms of her feet.

The landscape sizzles to orange, the green dying inwards
                               and heat-haze blurs the
sharpness of nature.
Dark skinned, she's lost among tunes harsh. The little
                               girl in her panics. Her native
tongue gets trapped amid a whirlwind of languages.
                               Fear needles prick her.
She's confused by a white god, brown god, yellow and
                               a black one.
Sun- stained, she quietly wears the tiara of thorns
                               disguised in Hibiscus.

Her continent is burnt and so is she. What remains are
                               shards of a *Third World*.

DAYBREAK

With a wooden spatula I flatten my heart,
the spilling music spirals outwards
leaving it toneless.
I say goodbye to all the sonorous voices.
Maybe, I'll arrive at a blank
maybe, I wont.
Like a shadow I will dissolve
among winter wheat,
doze among uncut flowers-restored.

From somewhere, a woodpecker will
alight on carbonic viruses and
discreet calculations, cleansing
the city bright.
Somewhere, in the universe the séance of
sterile hours will melt welcoming the
chastening influence of sleep.
Somewhere, the first notes of daybreak
will flood my heart.

Maybe…

DISTANCES

Distances are blurred horizons
and carries smell of ruined hills.
Distances create distance of their own
and arrival or departure repose in a mausoleum.
Distances are worlds unto themselves where everything
is orchestrated into a mirage-symphony of images.

FINDING ONESELF

This is the final call for all passengers…

The line beeped.
She hurried towards Gate A.
Her high heels hushed and muffled
in the thick carpeting. Her tote bag
wasn't heavy it had things beautiful
and annihilating.
There was a yellow scarf with black stripes-
a crouched tiger fanning fires that never expired.
She kept a copy of Ariel and forgot all about
the gas stove. The Waterman ink pen an extension
of her soul, when motivated spoke in soft secret tongue.

The world purred in her tote.

Again the digital line beeped.
She hurried on. She cared less for all the clouds pressing
in. Her movement was a witness to the ebullient star that
had been ignited.

DELHI 2010

The city's throat has been slit
and blood clots in inhospitable hollows,
there are cobwebs forming on its skin.

The city can't sleep for its catarrh.

It snores across multiplexes,
sports complexes,
housing estates and brothels.
Its scribbles and scrawls end up in
million dollar scam.
What happened to that charming face
that comes from a joyful heart?
What's the use of rain and foliage
when all the birds have
disappeared in warm tears?

The swarm of precision greenery
encircles the rich man's quarter.
Just beyond, women sit cold as rocks
their eyes stilled, singed by Lucifer.
Their children play with rickety legs
in the androgynous light.
Hunch- back questions get dissolved
in the emptiness of royal tombs and
age worn soil.

Under the sagging breast of history
the city limps to midnight blaze.

FORGETTING IS EASY

The day I could say *I*
and point out a finger and
say *you*, and within that day
we died.
I merrily forgot that day is
prefixed and suffixed by
night,
as light is by darkness.
I also forgot to look at your
eyes,
sad eyes where dreams fade out.
I was so immersed in parceling
earth, me and you,
that I totally forgot that there are
things,
which apparently not existing, exists-
decelerating and watering
 the inner self.

IF ONLY

If only time would trickle slow,
if only my bones wouldn't kindle like dry wood,
if only death and divinity weren't clubbed together.

If only
if only
if only…

Right at this moment I do not cherish this wishful thinking.
For nestling in my ready arms is a flame,
burning and blistering, banishing shadows
from under my breasts,
climbing all over my frame in delirium, in alchemy,
battering me, flattening me
and I am about to disappear.

SARNATH

In perfect silence and indolence
I walk between rows of ruins.
In the landscape of Sarnath
every stone is a Buddha
and each tree a *Bodhi-Briksha*.
Here time writes its own script
fighting the nettles and the
algebra of ideas.
Remembered history plays
snakes and ladders with
 intricate time.

The sun lighting the hollow spaces
of the terrain reopens forgotten
moments even if for once.

FOR FREIDA CALHO

Oh Freida who is fingering your shroud?
I can hear you coming, crossing the
old mansion's tower and can see your
dark braided hair with feathers,
your perfume drifting past and
settling on uncut flowers.
But before I embrace your form,
I want to see with eyes full of flint
the draperies and naked bodies
in perpetual chiaroscuro.
Flirting with your pigments, I want
to dab violet on the face of mist,
gore sorrow with a riot of crimson-scarlet
and fling viridian on the face of earth to
 be fresh again. Believe me I do not care
 how you handle your brush or
whether unknown empires rise in your canvas
 or knights and plebeians cross swords on
deserted highway.
I just want your blushing glow and
 whisk the Dark Angel into first light.

I WONDER

...there are in my heart furies and sufferings...
Quevedo

Have I said this before? Possibly not. I don't even know why I have opened my compose mail. Right click, left click. The sound gives me company. I am tired of your small games as I am tired of my shadow. At night I gaze at you in wonder, asleep, without a care in the world. What do you see when you close your eyes? Do you see the dust devouring our bodies? Have you seen my hand sliding down you filled with salt and blood or felt bodies turned to fossil, killed by history? Years have passed and all the subtleties have decomposed. The spaces between ourselves rank with the smell of mold. Can you count how many shades of poetry have become pathetic?

Why ask for more if you can't give me your hand? Outside the rain is splattering on the window pane. The marigold in my balcony are drooping. There is a great deal of things I wanted to tell you but most have become rancid. But one still remain-

Listen, I was there a witness even if you never arrived.

OH ALEXANDRIA

A few chipped beads
and humbled burnt bricks
groan in defiance
against wind and indifference.

The ancient city is no more.

Head so severed by cruel centuries
that not a prayer nor even icy chill
can make her look otherwise.
The city knew the odds on failure
from the start.
In the purple-pink of the evening
she saw her fragrant gardens and wells,
sheep and spices going down earth-chutes
and third- rate settlements
cropping on her foreskin
jamming her pores with concrete.

How many centuries ago
did the marketplace swell
with cotton bales and
the ships docking like a series
 of promises?
How many lives ago?
Was it yesterday?

There is no answer.

Under the windswept plain crisscrossed
by archaeologist's digging spree
the city-blood clots and
language turns to hieroglyphs.
Time whitewashes, coat after coat
till the passionate midnights find place
in museum halls.

COFFEE BAR

Tomorrow, perhaps, we shall sit
at the coffee bar reserving
a small black coffee and
Darjeeling tea.
Burt right now I am reserved for
twittering voices, celebrating
my secret poetry.
I realize that all poems
are basically dormant
until you flesh them
in denials and delights.
Words twirl with lucidity
devouring earth water fire air
and my imagined coffee gets cold.
The silent noon hangs over the city
and I long for coffee with cinnamon.

Perhaps, tomorrow we shall sit
at the coffee bar,
tomorrow, perhaps, at noon.

MUNDANE LITTLE THINGS

Holding onto life which is lined and dog-eared
is warm and comfortable. Plants in tiny earthen pots
on the verandah, patina covered furniture, clothes piled up
waiting to be pressed and the sound of pots and pans from the kitchen,
all have the essence of belonging.

The blinds get drawn as the midday heat rises
and the interior turns opaque. The smell of moisture
settles on the floor.
Mashed potatoes, steamed egg plant and tomatoes are
refrigerated, while dreams are thawed and lived.
Like mustard they have a sting that nudges you
from a stupor.
Bleary eyed you realize it is still late afternoon
and all the mundane little things
are imperishable- half closed stars
waiting for your touch.

RUINS

Naked and immense
The ruins stare at me.
Here the evenings are still born
children and the rain if falls at all is
light as a grasshopper.

I have my notions about other ruins,
but this one makes me search myself.
Each cry
I utter is lost in the limitless space
then it gathers speed and hits the
frozen walls breaking into an echo.

Perhaps, the story I'm looking for
is buried beneath the mosaics and
in the whispering of the lizards.
Perhaps,
it is there when the
first star shines and the
gods of night draw their curtain
over moon-drenched pillars.

SONG OF MOHENJODARO

There are stories that will not go away…

Black motifs burnt into my skin
stories that will not go away.
The spent years seeping out of me
falling crumbling to dust.

Mile after mile
over boulders and outcrops
The story continues-
It lays itself out plays hide and seek
to be searched again to be familiar yet new.

There are stories that will not go away
black motifs burnt into my skin.

MY VALENTINE

Words-sound-patterns
Words-images composed
whispering presence within me.
Sometimes, you are so quiet that
all I can foresee is a stale yoghurt sky,
dead stars and fat ladies wearing
diaphanous tunics that madden me.
Nevertheless, I love this also.
Shadows from houses, are toneless graphics
on the road, and my own image a phantom
with a scallop of lace where the neck
should have been.

But on certain days
you are like a speeding dart
wounding my phantom image,
urging me to wear a diadem of conquered shadows
and carving scripts for an unknown destination.

Words my valentine,
words my story,
just not a conjunction of
vowels and consonants
but my body and my tomb.

SLEEP-SMELL

The smell of your sleep fell upon my words
winding through kiosks and summer lanes.
It brushed over my sleep-languid lashes,
 travelled with me
and rested on the kitchen table.
All day the kitchen smelt of your sleep
turning radishes into white cedar javelins
and carrots, carnelians, the size of your thumb.
The smell bleeding and peeling, falling like
rain, like flakes on the kitchen floor
wove stories of *Geet Govinda* stretching
and interlacing with noon.
All day your sleep-smell smeared the air
then in a moment of tenderness
gushed out of the kitchen window
leaving behind traces of unheard-of lanes

SEA SHELL

I found a sea shell with the sea
lingering inside it.
Each night I place the shell
upon my pillow close to my ear.
Each night watery maps of continents
surface. Each night sun-warmed paths
of the earth dig deep in the soil from where
kernels of hope sprout.

But in the memory book of the sea there is
nothing, only waves- curvy, glistening,
synchronized with a mystic astronomy.

THE WRITTEN WORD

I have smelled the alphabets in my childhood,
each with a distinct flavour, made them cursive
and freezed them in my memory stamped
with my signature.

Like a sculptor my fingers created
slanting As, upright Bs, narrow Cs and
joined them to form word-landscape.
In the word-kitchen, my fingers like a master chef
combined words, soaked them in joys of black ink,
moments and prophecies and then in the
half light of early morning they became
tall grasses, barefoot walking, rain on the sea…

Now exiled from earth by the virtual,
the written word sits crouched, and world holding
a piece of antediluvian world
amid the impersonal sound of
texting, tapping, typing.

SEA

I have come back once again

Standing on a jutting land alone with the sea.
Enveloped again by sea patterns, my eyes softening,
 I learn from all my desires-
With age a body can hold a lot of secrets.
Each memory a photographic negative,
the waves come in and ebb away one by one.
The moments are liberated silhouettes against
breakers and the salty spray floods my cells
lifts me above the flash floods of love.
The effortless sea exhilarates me,
like a black hole sucks my soul.

I realize I'm the sea.

STOP

Stop. Along this path horsemen galloped conquered territories called continents. Defeated by history and amid chants you cannot fathom, you became a *barbarian*. Your theogony bombed and historiography side tracked, you lost all known taste only to become a stranger who embraces death without tears.

Now after eons of mornings you are still the same just that you have learnt to talk like them, dressed in their fatigues. Only when there is a dark cloud on the eastern horizon or perhaps, when the earth becomes tender with indolence and all the bed-time stories that your grandmother told you race across the savanna of your mind, you realize that even a bucket of rain in your unkempt backyard is better than *first world* landscaped garden.

Tropes For The Intelligent Man

LOVE

When love is just a word
formed by lips thick and thin,
multiple theories crop up
for the macabre dance to lean.

When love is tagged with labels
rituals, dry dreams and disguise,
every phone call is laboured
and love dies with decision sad- wise.

When love is stoned with stones of tears
and the heart defenseless, a weary whore,
no cry is ever too loud for the brute's ear
and the soul dies on a lonely shore.

When love is toughened with grimy indifference
and smeared with logic and the proper noun *I*,
all painting, all music start to disappear
and love becomes a worthy tool to lie.

FAITH

When faith is a soothing pretence
a game plan based on never ending need,
you can forget what your grandmother said
and rest assured you've sowed the right seed.

When faith is a beckoning lemon tree chimera
against the cool lemony shade,
you can gulp down Tom Collins at one go
congratulating that your matrix was well laid.

When faith is a merchandise bought and sold
in emails, behind closed doors and soft speech,
one can feel peaceful that nothing haunts the heart
there's absolutely nothing, nothing at all to teach.

When faith forgets about its outstretched hand
and fails to grasp the other dipped in hope,
it's a waltz between the albatross and the ancient mariner
which the intelligent man can surely cope.

PRETENCE

When pretence is all lace and chocolate
an angel with a dimpled cheek,
hug, embrace and coo amorous words
it will not do good to be meek.

When pretence is the very in thing
the costliest cosmetic that one can buy,
Flipkart and Amazon .in are flowing with orders
get up, tap your keyboard lest you fail and cry.

When pretence is an attractive lover
all caring and god great,
you cannot help but be in love
after all you were never straight.

When pretence becomes second nature
where what is real or make believe hard to tell,
the intelligent being feels overjoyed
while the gods above smile and say *well!*

PRAYER

When prayer is just a marker
a fashionable 21st century trope
it can be used in boardrooms and seminars,
to clothe disquiet with hope.

When prayer is just words and words
struggling for its deep dignity and reserve,
right then it is pickled more
bottled as new age preserve.

When prayer is just a sweet cover
for bloodshed, hatred and dark noise,
people at the top can sing hallelujah
without giving a damn to the other voice.

When prayer ceases to be a prayer
submerged under superlatives half true,
even then it is a mighty heavyweight
 without it what would the world do?

TRAIN LEAVES

The train left…

Twelve hours back I sat on my chair
and contemplated this moment.
Twelve hours from now each nano second
will be a vein throbbing in my forehead.
Time is measured by glimpses and unsaid words.
Each second is a downy form in the dying minute
and I am buoyed towards the zero hour.

SUNDAY NIGHT BLISS

Day after day night after night the sameness dulls her brain
who is to see who is to judge the numbness and the pain.
So she talked herself into a virtual reality for
she refused to see grief mirrored in her eyes
she knew all the circles and pentagons
of insipid assurances and lies.

She imagined herself in a time- machine. The fixed transparent glass panes reflected
mauve-gold, for here day and night ceased to exist. There was no god, no original sin.
Her words did not carry any sound and she focused her infinite telescope beyond the
mythology of time.
Such things took place in an eye blink.
Instinctively she lit a candle to warm the cold folds of her intuition. A smile fell on
her lap. Through the indigo amnesia of the universe her time-machine raced on.

Hold your breath and you can see
a shooting star or a fruit falling.
The sky waking from recent sleep
a voice calling softly calling.

She tossed her black head, stretched her toes on the soft rug and looked
at her own toe nails, warm and glossy. Her body a hot topography of tiered emotions was
melting into the hour of change. Her palms half open she reached out for the countless
flashes of mysteries adorning the unheard of horizon.

SONG

The street I walk have no name.
It has been wiped clean
and the sharpness and clarity
stand out against
little holes in the cement.
They come to life in the evening-
-hundred neon lights, hundred new moons.
                                    A lone door swings...

Cities flame and there are
separations within separations,
circles encircling circles
and I'm pushed subtly
                          to forbidden zones...

I forget all of these,
as a gentle breeze nudges me
and I pass by.
            Night spreads like beaten silver
touching hearts in search of something.
A bell tolls in the distance
and the earth eagerly waits
for the sound
that moves beneath the ocean
                            to fill life with a song.

T3

I went to T3, the tea bar, a landscape
of linear precision.
As before I waited forgetting that
the day was wrong, the week too early
and the year…

As before I ordered for two cups of tea.
As before I waited for you to pour the tea
little realizing that the chair opposite
was empty.

When you come (if at all)
possibly you will find the tea cups brimming-
two warring countries with an unnoticed border.

ONCE AGAIN

Things happen…
Earthquake
fire
flood.

Things happen…
Darkness and light
certitude and doubt
pain and radiant angel.
Things happen…

I have seen it all.

Now I watch with eyes softened with years
the rising morning caressing the earth crusted
 with scars, the cool shadow of ancient trees
knotting the landscape with a violet ribbon. And
 unexpectedly there arises grasshoppers all lime
decoding the secrets of the mountains
and parchments waiting to be used
where you could once again begin your day.

TRYING TIMES

It is a difficult time-
a tragic time.
The sun rises
but the blocks remain dark
and doubtful fingers half open
apartment doors with apprehension.
The newspapers are chronicles
of victims and villains.
Monday mornings are dark lines
interweaving the metropolis,
breaking into grids of
power and isolation.
Deep groans intersperse
the concrete, i pods and brain.
The boxy high rises are craters
holding heat.

But somewhere beyond
the octopus-growth
a fenceless world tries to
stand on crutches.

TURNIP

You are already turning into a turnip
in a landscape where the sky is rust magnet
and scars emerge magnified on the demented screen
of politics.
The hard casing of mediocrity leaves you intact.
Entombed in shameless vulgarity, your blatant life
fans out from room to roads to cities
 and power centers.

You feed with your eyes only.

But what if vibrations fermented in heaven
hits you in the eye, will you then write your
own script, unlock the gate of hypnotic siesta
and let lemon grass and thyme grow on your
front yard?
Will you then let anti-matter drop from ceiling
collapsing on the inner deck
of your thought?

VEILED

The manuscripts are well preserved
across generations in hieroglyphs, in eyes, in touch
and of course in bodies, broken, stabbed and salted.
A sickle and a hammer or a crescent and a lotus,
it does not matter.
What is left is a summer song lost in tidal waves.
What is left are our eyes
veiled in colourful cosmetic lenses.

We have all around us noises

darkening the rim of our lives.
The *twitter*, the *facebook* have seen to that.
We sit in the intimacy of a coffee bar only
to be jerked upright by the over- friendly mobile.
Nothing is private anymore,
fear, bent upside down, descends on us
in roaring spasms.
In this immeasurable darkness
the earth no longer remembers us.

So just tell me in this hour of need
how can we rip the veil
and offer ourselves to the
solitary raindrop?

WATER DROPS

This is no pulp fiction…

Let me be the water drops
dripping from your telephone shower.

Are you kidding?
No, no not at all.
Water is life
I'm life.
You may say that I've dreamed more
than I've worked.

Are you joking?

Whatever you think, it doesn't matter.
I surrender my heart to you.

Let me be the rivulets
that run along your body.
You see me but there is
nothing to be seen.
You feel me and your
senses are aroused.
You can't hold me
yet I'm there.
I've no colour, no smell
unless you choose to

perfume me with your
intimate odour.
Each morning
I'm a sort of a worship
and I love this ritual
of gliding uninterrupted,
softly sinking into your flesh,
waltzing to the tunes of some
far-off earthen flute.

POLITICIAN

Of course I'm opposed to what you say
colourful flatteries to win hearts.
Now that your secret is discovered
it litters the marketplace, public square and home.
The half stories and half lives you call negotiating
are nothing but narcotic crossovers.
At midnight when the candle slurs in soft wax
when faces blur, do you hack truth with
razor-sharp fingers? Does love die in your heart
before it has a chance to be a doing word?
Your mortal sight is vicious enough to leave
everything mutilated.
My hate is but a heap of shame that points
to deceptions.
So imagine your name, the alphabets bloated
with blood, cursive, against a white washed wall
extending in cunning malice to choke your throat
and the voice in your head dry enough to catch fire.

SHE II

There she was breathless with primeval rhythms, barefoot at your door.

She left the world behind for inner space. The hot sun reflecting a little lit up, dazzled and burnt her whole body. Gold-curved and trembling, reposed in forest-silence, she opened up to feed love.

SENTENCES

Sentences with liquid words debate within my head all
night
trying to find new harmonies and chords.
The warm-veined alphabets meditate with other
alphabets
within the organ pipes and steeples of my mind
in search of new words.

I watch curiously, soft-hard words gathering into
the depths of other words, purple cluster of sentences
blushing through my thoughts trying to capture
unpublished manuscripts.

LOOSING COLOUR

There is no dream
there is no oblivion.
I move slowly in a line of flight
blanched by dust and sand.
The air is rife with the words
smoke'em out, smoke'em out.
I have no one to talk to
everything is divided,
even my poetry book.
Each page, each friend is a dried butterfly
pasted beautifully, loosing colour.
I stagger rootlessly from one page to another.
I see a fire escape looming out of my anguish.
But where does it lead to?
Will it penetrate the mindless deceptions and
reveal unmirrored space?
Will it delete all those outsized disjointed words?
Will my grey heavy look get a twinkle?

There's no going back to childhood
and from childhood to the safety
of the womb.
I have no wish to be the silent hero of my life.
I write for you as I write for myself
even though you'll never read these words.

But watch out.
Someday the ants will attack.
There will be cloudburst and landless limbo
and when you open the door
a mummified hand of a child
will be there to greet you.

PILGRIMS

They speak I know of hallucinating angels
of feverish disorder in May
of secret language and old hate.
I also know they preach of dos and don'ts
to enter the gate of heaven.

As for myself I do not care
whether heaven or hell exists.
I want us to be pilgrims in search
of an unknown god who speaks of love
who is everywhere at once.

NIGHT

Through the humid stifling of the night,
darkness, sizzling swallowing light
gnarled dark concentrated lies
circles me, and poetry dies.

Pangs of pain, chill and long
I shiver, I flinch, I'm not strong
Under rumbling, burning, cracking sky
I rise and give the first infant's cry.

VOYAGE

Crossed legged on the floor
I open the first chapter on trade winds.
The warm fragrance of distant cities
and abandoned shells
waft over the loam of my being.
Before I know my eyes cut through
the twisting mist to the distant horizon.
Liquid notes of unheard melodies float by-
galleons, plazas and a fascinating time,
all freeze to take shape in a molten landscape.

On the other side you cannot
see the waves breaking against the cliff
nor hear the scraping of a broken scull
against the keel. You cannot even smell
the aloe, the cinnamon and clove
all floating in the cobalt water.

But I want you to do all these things.
I want to make you sit
on a rough sailcloth and
murmur words of love.
They would be hissing in the wind
like Casurina leaves.
We would build a fire and
cook supper among the
green bracken and moss.

This is nakedness.

As I reach you through
my word, my alphabet,
the alleys, the byways diminish.
And each sound of the keyboard
like a milestone recedes
taking me towards you.

WRITING A POEM IS NOT EASY

What a hard time I have composing a poem.
the words swoon and fall upon my stiff fingers.
Sometimes, they strut in line of my vision,
magnifying themselves into disjunct words.

My friends think writing a poem is easy-
White paper, thesaurus and a bit juggling
with phrases. I laugh inwards, for they have
overlooked the crooked light swathed with
white delirium. They only see the mirror without
clouds. They cannot hear the mirror calling softly
to occupy the blank space behind it.
They fail to understand that roots also
gaze at stars through pores in the soil.

Writing a poem is not easy.

Every day I sit and pray for words.
Everyday I'm tortured by words.
Words superimpose on my life every day.
Every day, wherever I go, I walk with words.

Buy at

www.hawakal.com

www.ingramcontent.com/pod-product-compliance
Lightning Source LLC
Chambersburg PA
CBHW031501040426
42444CB00007B/1165